Love Poems

For
Cards & Letters

Written By

Ara John Movsesian

Illustrations By
Marjorie Rodgers

The Electric Press
Fresno, California

Library of Congress Cataloging in Publication Data

Movsesian, Ara John.
    Love poems for cards & letters.

    Includes index.
    1. Love poetry.   2. Love-letters.   3. Greetings cards.
I. Title.   II. Title: Love poems for cards and letters.
PN6110.L6M68   1988   811'.54   88-81507
ISBN 0-916919-60-9   (pbk.)

Library of Congress Catalog Card Number 88-81507

Cover design by Ara John Movsesian

Printed in the United States of America
First Printing, September 1988

DEDICATED TO

**Ann and Hygus
Ed and Alice**

ACKNOWLEDGEMENTS

Acknowledgement is made to Marjorie Rodgers for the illustrations found in the Love Poem section.

Appreciation is expressed to Gene Garabedian, Rod Mazman, and Cynthia Movsesian for reviewing the manuscript.

The poems: "Our Day Will Come", "Happiness", "Needs", "Let's Compromise", "A Precious Love", "A Single Word", "Your Vision", and "Flying" were first published in Pearls of Love . Fresno, Calif. The Electric Press. ©1983.

TABLE OF CONTENTS

LOVE POEMS 1

Beginnings 3
Do You Care? 6
Friendship 7
Hope For The Future 9
I Am Happy! 11
If I Had A Wish 12
I Can't Live 13
I Love You! 14
I Miss You! 16
I Need You! 19
I Think Of You! 24
Just A Note 26
Let's Not Argue 28
Love Is 29
Our Love Is Strong! 33
Please Write! 35
Potpourri 37
Reconcilliation 41
Roses Are Red 43
Special Ocassions 45
To Cheer You Up 48
Valentine's Day 49
You Are Beautiful! 51
You Are Special! 53
You Are The Best! 57
You Attract Me! 58
You Make Me Feel Good! 60

APPENDIX A / *How To Make Your Own*
Personalized Greeting Card **65**

Step-By-Step Procedure 67

APPENDIX B / *Examples Of Love Letters*
With Poem Inserts **71**

Love Letter No. 1 - Beginnings 73
Love Letter No. 2 - Friendship 74
Love Letter No. 3 - Declaration of Love 75
Love Letter No. 4 - The Pain of Separation 76
Love Letter No. 5 - Reconcilliation 77
Love Letter No. 6 - Reaffirmation of Love 78

APPENDIX C / *Selected Love Symbols*
For Cards And Letters **79**

INDEX **85**

LOVE POEMS/Introduction:

Mass-produced greeting cards are great,
   When time is short and you are late;
With pictures and poems, they do excel,
   And they get the job done very well.

But if you really want to say
   "I love you" in a special way,
Buy a card with the inside blank -
   It's like putting money in the bank!

Then pick the poem which says it best -
   Those feelings which you need expressed;
And then write the poem down by hand,
   To make a card of your very own brand.

   The love poems in this little book were written especially for you -
to help you make your very own brand of romantic greeting card.
Use them as is or modify them to suit your own personal needs. You
can rearrange verses, expand short poems into larger ones, or in-
corporate certain verses into your own love poems. Some verses
even have alternate words which you can choose and then use.
These are found in parenthesis (). As you will see, the variations are
endless!
   The whole process is easier than you think and it works. Your
personalized greeting card will make a deep and lasting impression.
After all, the poem comes from your heart - through your own hand.
Now, how can a mass-produced greeting card beat that?!

Beginnings

That Special Night

It seemed as though I could not find
   The (*lovely/handsome*) vision in my mind;
That is, until that (*special/fateful/wondrous*) night,
   When you came walking into sight.

-❤-

My Feelings Changed

At first (*I could not stand/I did not like*) you,
   And I (*think/know*) you felt the same;
But now, every lonely night,
   Silently, I call your name.

-❤-

I Searched The World

I searched the world for you,
   Not knowing where you'd be;
But always hoping that one day,
   Your (*lovely/handsome*) face I'd see.

A Chance Encounter

A chance encounter of the best kind -
    A meeting arranged by fate;
Whatever you choose to call it,
    I think we should celebrate!
So come with me next (*day of the week*) night
    And get to know me more;
We'll eat and drink beneath the stars
    And laugh while we explore.

-❤-

The First Time

The first time I saw you
    A rush of excitement
        Flooded my senses,
And for once
    In my life
        I had no defenses.

-❤-

My Daffodil

You are a lovely Daffodil,
    Sitting temptingly on a hill;
While I, a Monarch butterfly,
    Search for nectar from the sky.

An Earthquake

Like an earthquake
  From down deep within,
Of a magnitude
  Too large to say;
A love which never
  Have I felt before
Jarred my (*heart/senses*)
  (*One/The*) (*lovely/special/lonely/other*)day.

-♥-

Feelings Of Love

There are many feelings stirring strong
  Deep within my heart;
Telling me that finally
  Love has made its start.

-♥-

Our First Embrace

Mighty rivers start from springs,
  And springs begin with small flakes of snow;
Thus hopefully our first embrace
  With patience and some (*luck/work*) will grow
Larger and larger into a true love
  Which binds our hearts and then imparts
To both of us the greatest joy
  That life could (*give/offer*) a grown girl and boy.

Do You Care?

Where Do I Stand?

I do not know just where I stand,
  Whether you love me - whether you care;
And so, I need to hear firsthand
  That I'm not just a brief affair.

-❤-

Are You Sincere?

You say to me "I love you!"
  But are you truly sincere?
For your actions do not confirm —
  Nor are your intentions clear.

-❤-

Do You Care?

Do you care for me as you say —
  Is the love we share (*divine/sublime*)?
Do you care for me as you say —
  Or is it your standard line?

Friendship

My Dependable Friend

I thank God each and every day,
  For giving me a (*constant/caring*) friend,
Whose friendship will not fade away -
  A friend on whom I can depend.

-❤-

A Special Friend

You are a (*true/caring*) friend who gives me much —
  Who's there to listen; Who's there in a clutch;
A friend like you is rare indeed —
  A Godsend and a special breed.

-❤-

I Am Lucky

I feel so very (*fortunate/lucky*)
  To have a friend like you,
Who is thoughtful, kind and giving,
  And loyal through and through.

A Wish For My Friend

You have proven to me firsthand,
  That you will always stand
At my side, in times of good - in times of woe,
  In rain or sleet or sun or snow;
And so I send this special wish,
  To a friend for a friendship
I will always cherish;
  May your life be filled with excellent health,
Much success and a bit of wealth;
  And may you live by the light above,
And feel the joys that come from love.

-❤-

Thanks!

Thank you for your (*thoughtfulness/confidence*),
  And your caring ways;
Thank you for your friendship,
  All these many days.

-❤-

My Friend

What would my life be without a friend —
  A buddy, a chum, a comrade?
A pal to laugh with and to cry with,
  In times of good or bad.
What would my life be without a friend?
  That day, I pray, I'll never see —
That day I hope will never (*be/come*),
  For I have one and you are (*he/she*).

8

Hope For The Future

Our Day Will Come

My dearest love, be not so glum,
  Our day of joy will surely come;
The (*torments which/pain and sorrow*) we felt before,
  Will fade away and hurt no more.

-❤-

A Brighter Day

Just as Winter gives way to Spring,
  So shall (*your/our*) troubles go away;
For time and faith in God will bring
  The dawning of a brighter day.

-❤-

A Happier Tommorrow

Right now, all things look bad,
  And life has little taste;
And yes, I know that you are sad
  And feel that trying is a waste;
But don't despair because life's unfair,
  The future is yours to mold;
So set your mind and someday you'll find
  (*Your personal pot of/A love as precious as*) gold.

9

Sweet Summer, Autumn, Winter, Spring;
Again, I know, your love will bring,
Like countless flowers on rolling hills,
A multitude of joys and thrills.

I Am Happy!

Joy, No. 1

My world is filled with joy these days;
    A joy that (*swells/comes*) from deep within;
(*Nourished/Nurtured/Fostered*) by the knowledge of
    Your deep and everlasting love.

-❤-

Joy, No. 2

What (*beauty/passion*) you possess;
    What charms you do employ;
To bring me happiness —
    To give me so much joy.

-❤-

Happiness

You give to me a tender love,
    Which surely comes from (*God/the Lord*) above;
Thus words can never quite convey,
    The happiness I feel each day.

If I Had A Wish!

Wish No. 1

If I had but one wish —
   My wish would surely be,
To have you here,
   With your arms around me.

-❤-

Wish No. 2

If I had one wish —
   That wish would be;
To reunite myself
   With thee.

-❤-

Wish No. 3

If I was given one wish —
   One wish I knew would come true;
I would wish with all my heart,
   For a rendezvous with you.

I Can't Live...

Without You

I can't live another day
  Without your (*lovely/smiling*) face;
I can't live another hour
  Without your warm embrace;
I can't live another minute
  Without your fiery kiss;
I can't live another second
  Without the one I miss.

-❤-

A Different Theme

I can't live as I did
  For my life has changed —
I can't live as I did
  For love has arranged
A different menu - a different scheme;
  A different tune - a different theme.

-❤-

You Make Me Complete

I cannot live without your love —
  My life would not be the same;
For I would be incomplete,
  Like a candle without a flame.

I Love You!

I Love You, No. 1

I love you - I love You - I love you;
   I could say it in millions of ways,
And thus, my hope is that you and I,
   Will be (*lovers/together*) for millions of days.

-❤-

I Love You, No. 2

You are the ultimate - supreme
   Fulfillment of my every dream;
Thus with these words I want to say,
   I love you more each passing day.

-❤-

Each Day Is Special

Each day of my life is special;
   Each day is a celebration!
Each day is filled with (*love/excitement*)
   And much anticipation.

I Love You, No. 3

Je t'aime! Je t'aime! Je t'aime!
  Yes kez shahd guh seerem!
And even though, you may not know
  The words I've used above,
They merely state what's in my heart -
  I love you! I love you!, my love!

-❤-

Love Has Grown

I have worked with you;
  Talked and laughed with you;
Shared life with you;
  And because of these special times
I have grown
  To love you.

-❤-

I Love You, No. 4

I can say many things to you,
  To tell you how I feel;
For instance, "I adore you!"
  Or, "You cook a tasty meal!"
But none of these confess,
  What is truly true;
Nor do they express,
  How much I really love you!

I Miss You!

Loneliness

With you away, the hours creep;
  My loneliness runs very deep;
My heart, dear love, can only weep —
  While I'm awake - while I'm asleep.

-❤-

I See Your Vision

I've been thinking of you constantly,
  At work - at home - asleep;
Your vision is all that I can see -
  Etched in my mind very deep.

-❤-

My Life Is Gray

I can't enjoy a lonely meal,
  Nor music do I wish to play,
For my life has lost all its color,
  With you so far away.

How much I truly miss you —
My words cannot express;
For deep within my heart
Is the greatest emptiness.

MARJORIE RODGERS

A Lovers' Rendezvous

Each night my visions wander far,
  To a place I cannot travel to;
And there they mingle with your thoughts,
  In a lovers' rendezvous.

-❤-

Separation

No proper words exist
  To describe the pain I bear
Whenever we are forced apart
  By (*twists/the hands*) of fate unfair.

-❤-

I Miss You, No. 1

My love, to you, I must confess —
  I miss you very much!
I miss your kiss! I miss your hug!
  I miss your tender touch!

-❤-

I Miss You, No. 2

Whenever many miles divide,
  I from you and you from me;
My thoughts constantly focus on,
  How much I miss your company.

I Need You!

I Need You

My passions soar from high to higher;
  My heart is filled with deep desire;
My (*situation/dilemma*) is pretty dire —
  I need you here to quench this fire!

-❤-

Return To Me

Each day you are (*away/apart*) from me,
  Seems (*longer/greater*) than eternity;
Your (*quick/safe*) return is my only plea,
  So I'll be rid of this agony.

-❤-

I'm Drowning!

I'm drowning in an ocean deep,
  Without a life raft near;
If only you could hear my pleas
  And rescue me, my dear.

A Dependency

Without your love, my life would be
   Wracked with pain and misery;
For I have a dependency
   Which needs fulfillment constantly.

-♥-

You Make Me Whole

Ever since you left that day,
   Loneliness has taken its toll,
For you are a part of all I am,
   And without you I am not whole.

-♥-

I Need Your Love

I need you now more than ever before,
   To help me in these times of (*stress/duress*),
By giving me your (*calming/soothing/precious*) love
   And with it much happiness.

-♥-

What Would I Be?

What would the Yin be without the Yang —
   What would Lemon pie be without the meringue?
What would false be without true —
   And what would I be without you?

You Are My Passion

How can I describe what you are to me?
 Mere words do you no justice -
For you are an infatuation which does not end -
 A fascination of the nth degree -
A passion which consumes all thought and deed
 And fills my life with (*poetry/ecstacy*).

-❤-

You Are Perfection

Without your loving affection,
 My life would be filled with (*dejection/depression*);
For you are a mirror reflection
 Of all that is truly perfection.

-❤-

I'm Lost!

I'm lost! I'm lost! There is no hope —
 I cannot find your guiding rope;
I wander all around and mope;
 In search of your love, I grope! I grope!

-❤-

A Gloomy Place

My world would be a gloomy place -
 A barren desert - an empty space -
Without your (*cheerful/sexy*), smiling face;
 Without your tender, warm embrace.

An ocean - a mile - a yard - a foot;
Even an inch is too much space,
When it keeps me from your tender touch
And the pleasure of your warm embrace.

Confession

By your charm and quick wit,
   I am impressed;
By your beauty and grace,
   I am obsessed;
By the thought of your love,
   I am possessed;
For (*months/years*) these feelings,
   I have suppressed;
But now, at last, they are expressed;
   At last, I have confessed;
At last, my mind can rest.

-❤-

Needs

I (*want/need*) to hold you in my arms,
   And (*partake of all/enjoy all of*) your charms;
I (*want/need*) to hear your loving sighs,
   And gaze into your (*sexy/dreamy/lovely*) eyes.

-❤-

Yearning

Something from deep inside me yearns
   For that which only you possess;
Thus, without you I could never hope
   To realize true happiness.

I Think Of You!

You Fill My Thoughts

You and only you, my love,
   Are in my thoughts today;
For nothing else is strong enough
   To make you go away.

-❤-

Dreams

Oh Lord! What (*loveliness/a handsome man*) I see
   Each time your vision fills my mind;
I am overcome by a passion deep -
   An urgent yearning which makes me blind;
And for a (*moment/time*), I forget
   That we are lovers torn apart;
And on to sunrise from sunset,
   I quench the fires within my heart.

-❤-

Thoughts

As I sit here alone,
   All my thoughts turn to you,
And my heart begins to race
   At the thought of a rendezvous.

The Thought Of You

My body and my spirit
   Are (*charged/filled*) with energy;
At the very thought of you
   And the love you have for me.

-❤-

I Dream

At night I lie in bed awake,
   And think of all your many charms,
And dream that someday you will be,
   Back safe in my loving arms.

-❤-

Point Of View

Your vibrant love lights up my mind,
   And fills my thoughts with you;
Giving my day a (*special/different*) look,
   From a (*special/different*) point of view.

-❤-

Thoughts And Passions

Even the briefest separation,
   Is very painful for me to take;
For I am flooded with thoughts of you,
   As well as passions I cannot shake.

Just A Note

Just A Note, No. 1

Just a note to tell you,
  How much you mean to me;
How much my life would suffer
  Without your company.

-❤-

Just A Note, No. 2

Just a note to tell you,
  How much I love your smile;
How much I love your humor —
  How much I love your style.

-❤-

Just A Note, No. 3

Just a note to tell you,
  That I enjoyed our date;
The food was good —
  The dancing better —
And you were really great!

Just A Note, No. 4

Just a note to say,
 I love you night and day;
I love you every moment —
 At home! At work! At play!

-❤-

Just A Note, No. 5

Just a note to wish you,
 Happiness and good health;
And a life filled with Love,
 Great success and wealth.

-❤-

Just A Note, No. 6

Just a note to thank you,
 For all that you have done for me;
For all your sacrifices,
 And for your loyalty.

-❤-

Just A Note, No. 7

Just a note to thank you
 For the love you give to me;
For the way you make my (*day/life*)
 A joyous certainty.

Let's Not Argue!

Trust And Honesty

My love, we started to drift apart,
   As ice upon the Arctic Sea;
When our love began to melt,
   With the loss of trust and honesty.

-❤-

Let's Compromise

True understanding must prevail,
   So that our love will never fail;
And if our thoughts don't harmonize,
   We both should try to compromise.

-❤-

Respect

True love can only exist
   If a man and woman reflect
Through their actions everyday
   The simple virtue of respect.

Love Is ...

Love Means...

"To love" means really "to respect";
   Never ever (*"to suspect"*/*"to inspect"*),
Or even slightly "to neglect",
   But "to nurture" - "to protect".

-❤-

Love Is A Force Field

Love is a force field which attracts
   Two solitary souls,
And binds them in a state of bliss,
   Away from (*opposing*/*opposite*) poles.

-❤-

Love Is A Force

Your love is a mighty, moving force,
   Which stirs my very soul;
And with its power, it will make
   My life complete and whole.

Your Love Is A Beacon

Your love is like a candle flame,
  Splitting darkness with its light -
A beacon showing me the way,
  To endless pleasure and delight.

-❤-

Love Is Like A Mountain Stream

Your love is like a mountain stream,
  Flowing from an endless spring;
To give my thirsty world a drink -
  To cause my heart to sing!

-❤-

Love Is Like A Spring Bouquet

Your sweet and everlasting love,
  Is like a Spring bouquet;
It is a gift from (*God/the Lord*) above,
  Special in every way.

-❤-

Love Is Like A Diamond

Our love is like a diamond
  Whose brilliance will not fade;
Time will never take its toll,
  For it is Heaven-made.

Love Is Great

It is true that our love is a meeting of minds;
   A touching of hearts;
And a merging of souls;
   But our love is also much greater
Than all of its separate parts.

-❤-

Love Is Contentment

Love is a symphony without notes;
   An artistic masterpiece without paint;
A classic sculpture without clay;
   Love is also contentment without complaint.

-❤-

Love Is Serenity

True love, by nature, is pristine;
   It works in countless ways unseen,
And gives to life a vibrant sheen,
   Which helps make inner lives serene.

-❤-

A Definition Of Love

If you take the words forgive,
   Understand, endure and trust;
If you add to each an "i-n-g,"
   You will get a definition of
What (*our/your*) love means to me.

The recipe of Love must always include
  Some herbs and spices for fortitude;
A tablespoon of forgiveness -
  A clove of loyalty -
A cup of faith -
  And a sprig of honesty;
A pinch of patience -
  A teaspoon of trust -
A cup of friendship -
  And a bit of lust;
Mix all these herbs and spices well -
  No other recipe could ever excel;
Add a man and a woman for proper effect;
  Then sauté the whole in two cups of respect.

Our Love Is Strong

A Precious Gift

The sweet love which you give to me,
   Is a precious gift from your heart;
I cherish it and promise thee
   That never will we split apart.

-❤-

My Love Grows

You are exciting and refined,
   (*Devoted/Unselfish*) and sincere;
And so, my love grows stronger
   With every passing year.

-❤-

A Precious Love

I reaffirm my love for you,
   And once again proclaim it true;
Thus never will the miles subdue,
   This precious love I have for you.

Our Love Is Strong, No. 1

Our love is based on truth and trust —
   Selfishness and jealousy do not belong,
For faith, forgiveness, and respect,
   Make our love very strong.

-❤-

Indestructable Love

Nothing in this earthly world
   Could ever destroy our love,
For it is bound by trust and faith
   In (*almighty God/the Lord*) above.

-❤-

Our Love Will Stand

Our love is built on solid stone,
   Unlike some others built on sand;
Thus when the storms of life unfold,
   Our love will always stand.

-❤-

Our Love Is Strong, No. 2

Each time I am away from you,
   I realize how much I care;
How much I need you at my side,
   And how strong is the love we share.

Please Write ...

A Single Word

For many days, I have not heard
    From you, my love, a single word;
Have you forgotten I exist,
    Or did you break your writing wrist?

-❤-

Silence

The silence of your pen
    Makes me deaf with despair;
Causing me to fear
    That you no longer care.

-❤-

My Bridge

Your letters were my only bridge,
    To a world I cannot see;
And when you stopped,
    My bridge collapsed,
In a heap of agony.

The Swallow

I search the skies for a Swallow;
   A bird which flies to lands afar;
In hopes that it will bring to me
   Some news of how you are.

-❤-

Passages

Words can loving friendships make,
   For words are windows to the mind;
And passages from heart to heart -
   Words can truly bind.

-❤-

Welcome Words

I know it's hard for you to write,
   When proper words are just not there;
But any words are a welcome sight,
   And make my (*dreary/stormy*) day turn fair.

-❤-

Your Letter

No longer do your letters come;
   I wait and wait and wonder why —
And when I send an inquiry,
   Silence is your cruel reply;
I guess just what they say is true,
   That out of sight is out of mind;
But way down deep I still have hope,
   That soon, your letter I will find.

Potpourri

Actions

Sometimes I can't express to you
    In words, how much you mean to me;
So with this verse, I want to say,
    That actions are my specialty.

-❤-

The Love Test

Each day tests our love -
    Is it true or false?
Is it a faddish dance step,
    Or a timeless waltz?

-❤-

Thrilled At Love

You cannot know how thrilled I was,
    When you confessed to me your love;
For as you spoke, my (*heart flew high/senses soared*)
    Up to - and through the clouds above.

Onto the Sea I sailed my boat,
   And prayed that it would stay afloat;
From dawn till dusk - from dusk till dawn,
   In search of love, I drifted on;
What happened then, I don't recall —
   I think it was a sudden squall;
For when I awoke, I thought I'd died,
   At the sight of an Angel at my side;
But lucky for me that was not true,
   For I'd found love and love was you.

Love Unites

It's hard for me to put in words
　　How much you really mean to me;
For words could never quite convey
　　The depth and purity
Of the love which binds our hearts
　　And fills our lives with warmth and sun,
Uniting all our separate parts -
　　And making our spirits one.

-❤-

The Promise

Your letters really make my day;
　　They always chase the blues away,
And bring to me the promise of
　　A future filled with endless love.

-❤-

I'm Here

Whenever you are feeling blue;
　　Whenever you need a hand or two;
Whenever troubles do ensue;
　　Just (*bear in mind/remember*), I'm here for you.

-❤-

Our Feelings Will Grow

Just as an Acorn will one day be,
　　A mighty Oak - a stately tree;
I (*know/hope*) the feelings which we share,
　　Will grow into a love quite rare.

Certainty

I wish! I want! I need! I yearn!
  For you, these (*feelings/thoughts/passions*) within me burn;
And only when our (*arms/hearts/vows*) entwine,
  Will I be certain you are mine.

-❤-

Lonely Isolation

My heart is locked behind a vault,
  In lonely isolation;
And you alone possess
  The (*only/needed*) combination.

-❤-

Pathways

There are many pathways on this Earth;
  Some lead to the mountains —
Some lead to the Sea;
  Some are quite expensive —
Some are totally free;
  There are many pathways on this Earth;
This, I know you can see —
  But the only pathway I hope you take,
Is the pathway which leads straight to me.

Reconcilliation

What Can I Say?

What can I say in my behalf —
   What words can I employ?
To heal the hurt I've caused;
   To make you smile with joy.

-❤-

Yearning

I am a (*tired/weary*) traveler,
   Far away from house and home;
Yearning to return to you;
   No longer (*wanting/wishing*) to roam.

-❤-

A Dulling Ache

Within my heart a dulling ache
   Reminds me of the big mistake
Which I once made when I left you
   To chase a love which proved untrue.

Sometimes words can be obstacles,
   As real as any mountain chain,
Or raging river running swift;
   Sometimes words can cause great pain
And create a lover's rift;
   But words can also fix bridges
      And heal wounds;
Words can spirits lift;
   And so with this verse, I send
My sincerest lover's gift —
   To cause the pain you feel to end;
To right the wrong of words untrue;
   From my heart - three words to mend;
And they are simply - I love you!

Roses Are Red

Roses Are Red, No. 1

Roses are red —
   Carnations are white;
You are (*such/truly*)
   A (*lovely/handsome*) sight.

-❤-

Roses Are Red, No. 2

Roses are red —
   Roses are white;
I think of you
   Both day and night.

-❤-

Roses Are Red, No. 3

Roses are red —
   Bluebells are blue;
My world was blessed
   When God made you.

Roses Are Red, No. 4

Roses are red —
  Magnolias are white;
Let's get together
  Later tonight!

-❤-

Roses Are Red, No. 5

Roses are red —
  Orchids are white;
I dream of you
  Most every night.

-❤-

Roses Are Red, No. 6

Roses are red —
  Gardenias are white;
I can't wait
  To hold you (*tonight/each night*).

-❤-

Roses Are Red, No. 7

Roses are red —
  Roses are pink;
Our love is stronger
  Than (*you/we/they*) think.

Special Occasions

Proclamation

I can't believe it's been (*twelve months/No of years*),
   Ever since that (*glorious/special*) day;
When you and I proclaimed a love
   Which will never fade away.

-❤-

A Happy Year

Twelve months have flown - my love has grown,
   It's been a (*happy/special*) year;
For you have been (*delightful/so loving*)
   (*Caring/Devoted*) and sincere.

-❤-

A Special Ocassion

A special occasion
   Is a special moment of life
Requiring a special wish
   For a special husband
From a loving wife —
   Ask me what it is, tonight!

As water flowing to the sea,
　Another year has come to be;
And so, on this most special day,
　From deep within my heart, I pray
That you will see Love's guiding light
　And follow it to me (*this/each*) night.

A Special Treat

My love, (*another year/No. of months*) (*has/have*) passed,
   Since you and I did meet;
And so on this most special day,
   I've planned a special treat!

-❤-

Happy Birthday!

I send this verse to you, my sweet,
   To express my deepest love,
And wish you a Happy Birthday,
   And health from (*God/the Lord*) above.

-❤-

I Wish!

I wish I could be at your side
   On this most special day;
To hold you and to kiss you,
   And love the night away.

-❤-

To Chase Your Blues Away

I know you're feeling quite depressed;
   It always happens on this day;
Thus I send this special thought
   To chase your blues away.
You are and you will always be
   As from the day of your birth —
The (*fairest/handsomest*) and the best —
   The (*loveliest gal/most wonderful man*) on Earth.

To Cheer You Up

A Little Keepsake

This little keepsake of my love,
  I send to you this day;
To brighten up your spirit
  And chase the blues away.

-♥-

I Care

I send this verse to cheer you up —
  To let you know I care;
To help you rise up through and above,
  Life's darkness and despair.

-♥-

Suggestion

I hate to see you feeling blue —
  I cannot bear the sight!
So I suggest some medicine
  To help you through the night.
I'll bring the prescription over, tonight!

Valentine's Day

For All The Times

For all the times I should have said
  "I Love You Very Much";
For all the times I should have given you
  A reassuring touch;
I do not make excuses now
  On this great day of Love;
But ask for your forgiveness,
  As (*God/the Lord*) looks on above.

-❤-

Separation

(*Dear/Dearest*) (*Valentine/Name*), my love runs deep;
  And so when we are forced apart,
I find it very hard to keep
  From crying deep within my heart.

-❤-

My Priceless Valentine

(*Dear/Dearest*) (*Name*), I must confess —
  A Valentine as (*sweet/nice*) as you,
Is quite unique and priceless,
  And a pleasure to pursue.

Reaffirmation

This fourteenth day of the second month,
  I reaffirm to you, my dear,
How much you really mean to me—
  How much I need you (*near/here*).

-❤-

Just Knowing

Just knowing that you exist,
  Makes my world divine;
Could it be that love has grown
  Between us, Valentine?

-❤-

Thrills

When you take me in your arms,
  You send a quiver up my spine;
Then you thrill me even more,
  (*Each time/When*) you kiss me, Valentine.

-❤-

A Loving Experience

To a (*charming/handsome*) Valentine,
  Who has made my life
A loving experience
  Filled with the joy of sharing
And much caring.

You Are Beautiful!

Beauty

At times, when you are not aware,
  I (*look/gaze*) at you discretely,
And when I do, I marvel
  At the beauty (*that I see/there before me*).

-❤-

Lovely Eyes

Your silken hair can entrance;
  Your stunning smile can hypnotize;
And both, together, do enhance
  The beauty of your lovely eyes.

-❤-

Endless Inspiration

If Heaven had a (*special place/gallery*),
  To display its most wondrous creation;
Your portrait would be there enshrined,
  As a source of endless inspiration.

There is much beauty
  On this Earth —
In stately trees
  And cloud-filled skies;
But the greatest beauty
  I've ever seen
Is found
  In your lovely eyes.

You Are Special

So Debonaire

You are so worldly and aware;
  I like a (man/gal) so debonaire;
You live your life with such a flair,
  That I consider you quite rare.

-❤-

My Greatest Find

You think I do not love you —
  How could you be so blind?
What must I do to make you see
  That you are my greatest find.

-❤-

Spring Flowers

There are countless flowers growing;
  Attracting - enticing - seducing;
But you, of all, are most pleasing —
  The fairest flower of Spring.

The Greatest Prize

With magnetic eyes that hypnotize;
　　With heavenly lips that tantalize;
You truly are the greatest prize,
　　That I could ever realize.

-❤-

Good Fortune

I (*am/feel very*) fortunate to have,
　　A loving, caring (*man/gal*) like you,
Who knows the secret of (*success/happiness*);
　　Who's gentle, (*strong/sincere*) and true.

-❤-

Ambrosia

You are a Rose among the weeds;
　　A diamond encircled by coal;
The Sun surrounded by night;
　　The Ambrosia of my soul.

-❤-

One-Of-A-Kind

You are someone special —
　　You are quite unique;
You are one-of-a-kind,
　　In mind and in physique.

The Answer

You are the answer to my prayer;
  You are the (*man/gal*) for whom I care;
For one like you so warm and kind,
  Is truly a rare and precious find.

-❤-

Exploration

You are a true temptation —
  A wondrous fascination!
A sensory stimulation
  Which (*needs much exploration/gives much inspiration*).

-❤-

Ecstacy

You are my Alexander;
  My brave Marc Antony;
When you hold me in your arms,
  I feel such ecstacy!

-❤-

On My Mind

You are easy to talk to,
  Understanding and very kind;
You are charming and disarming,
  And always on my mind.

Without you near, my world would be
A cold and lonely wilderness;
For you are my key to ecstacy,
And my bridge to happiness.

MARJORIE RODGERS

You Are The Best!

Nothing Better

Rodin would be hard-pressed to find
  A better model for his art;
As I would be to find in life
  A better (*consort/comrade/companion*) for my heart.

-❤-

Three Words

In life, there are three words —
  Good and better and best;
Good is good and better is better —
  But you, my love, are best!

-❤-

Pearls

There are many, many pearls in the Sea;
  Most are flawed to some degree;
But of all that are, and will ever be —
  You are the most perfect pearl for me.

You Attract Me!

Opposites

You are North and I am South;
  True opposites are we;
And yet our hearts attract
  Like magnets - forcefully!

-♥-

A Charm So Strong

It's hard to keep my mind on work
  With you so close to me each day;
For you possess a charm so strong
  That it draws my thoughts away.

-♥-

Love Power

I feel the power of your love,
  Wherever I may be;
It gives me an inner strength,
  Which helps me constantly;
I feel the power of your love,
  Showing me the way
To happiness and contentment
  Each and every day.

A Magnet

Your beauty is a magnet;
  My mind is made of steel;
For when you pass my (*office/desk*),
  You cause my thoughts to reel.

-❤-

Out Of My Mind

When you walk into the room
  I can't help noticing your
    Lovely lips and exotic perfume —
Your alluring eyes and (*graceful/sexy/sensual*) figure —
  All of which work together
    To drive me
      Out of my mind.

-❤-

Starship

You are like a starship,
  Sailing out into space;
Pulling me along
  In your tractor beam's embrace.

-❤-

Words

Whenever I am alone with you,
  I can't find the right words to say
How irresistible you are to me,
  And how you've swept my heart away.

You Make Me Feel Good

Pleasure

A (*handsome/lovely*) face like yours
   Is but a work of art;
To gaze at it gives me pleasure,
   And stimulates my heart.

-❤-

Refreshment

Your eyes are sparkling pools of blue;
   They refresh me with their calming hue;
And always they, somehow, renew
   My battered spirit through and through.

-❤-

Sensual Delight

You are without a doubt,
   A truly (*lovely/handsome*) sight,
And a constant source
   Of sensual delight.

Your Vision Delights

The vision of your (*handsome/lovely*) face,
    Occupies a most special place;
Where always ready to delight —
    It shows itself each lonely night.

-❤-

You Lift My Spirits

You are the sunshine of my life;
    You lift my spirits high;
With joy unbound, you give to me,
    A love to fill the sky.

-❤-

Warm Caress

Whenever I am filled with stress,
    I crave your soothing, warm caress;
For when I'm in your firm embrace,
    My stress departs without a trace.

-❤-

Knowing

Nothing on Earth
    Makes me feel better
Than the warmth of your touch,
    And the thought of knowing
That you love me very much.

Sensation

The very moment I met you,
   I felt a new sensation;
From deep within my heart —
   A heavenly vibration!

-❤-

Flying

You touched me just the other day,
   Quite gently - in a special way;
My body quivered - my senses swirled,
   My heart flew half-way 'round the world.

-❤-

A Dream

I have waited for a long, long time,
   To (*find/meet*) a (*man/gal*) like you;
Who makes each day worth living,
   And each night a dream come true.

-❤-

Golden Wings

My heart is an Eagle soaring high,
   Through a cloudless sky above;
Riding currents of (*delight/happiness*),
   On golden wings of Love.

Meaning

Whenever you return to me,
  No longer does my heart despair;
For you give meaning to my life,
  And make me feel like a millionaire.

-❤-

A Natural High

Booze or drugs, I do not need
  To cause my mind to fly;
For all I need is you,
  To reach a natural high.

-❤-

Wondrous Feelings

I see you every day
  As you walk in
    Through the door;
And each time, you stir
  Within me wondrous
    Feelings
Which never have I felt
  Before.

-❤-

You Send Me ...

Whenever you embrace me —
  Each time your lips touch mine;
You send me to (*Valhalla/Paradise*),
  To a wondrous land divine.

63

A Pleasant Sight

You have a (*handsome, rugged/cute, delightful*) face;
   You have a tender heart of gold;
You're a joy to kiss and embrace,
   And a pleasant sight to behold!

-❤-

Butterflies

Every time you call on me,
   My heart begins to race;
Butterflies begin to stir,
   Especially when we embrace.

-❤-

My Haven

When at last my eyes meet yours,
   And my arms embrace your (*lovely/handsome*) form;
Only then will I feel safe
   From the (*ravages/pain*) of my life's worst storm.

-❤-

Seasons

My life is made of seasons strong;
   Some are short and others are long;
Some are joyous and some are sad;
   Yet, through each season - good or bad,
Just knowing that you are always there,
   Makes me feel like a millionaire!

APPENDIX A/How To Make
Personalized Greeting Cards

Introduction

Anyone can go to a local card shop and buy a romantic greeting card. There are literally thousands to choose from, and as I mentioned earlier, many are well done with poignant sayings.

In recent years, however, blank greeting cards have become more prevalent. Most have cover pictures and a few are blank altogether. These cards have begun to address our needs for personalized expression. Indeed, there is nothing more powerful than a card with a romantic saying written in the sender's own handwriting.

The following step-by-step procedure will show you how to create your own personalized greeting card using inexpensive materials and the poems contained in this volume.

Procedure

Step #1: Purchase a blank card. If the card already has a picture on it, go directly to step #7. If it is completely blank, go on to step #4.

Note: If a blank card is not available, obtain some construction paper or card stock 8-1/2"x11" in size. Any color is acceptable although white is more versatile.

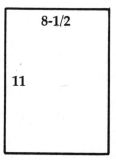

Step #2: Cut the paper down to 7"x10" in size.

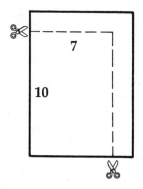

Step #3: Fold the 7"x10" paper in half.

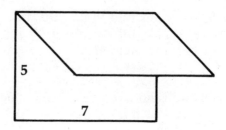

Step #4: Obtain some art work for placement on the front of the card. There are several ways you can do this. 1) You may photocopy the art from Appendix C: Selected Love Symbols; 2) You may draw in your own artwork; or 3) You may use gift wrap.

Note: If you use gift wrap, make sure that it represents pictorially or with words the ocassion you are concerned with (ex. Valentine's wrap for romantic cards, Birthday wrap for birthday cards, etc.).

Note: You may wish to wrap a gift first and then use the same gift wrap for the greeting card art work.

Step #5: When using gift wrap for the art work, cut out a small section in the form of a square, rectangle or circle.

Step #6: Attach the cut section of gift wrap (or photocopied artwork) to the front of the blank card using double stick tape or stick glue.

Step #7: Select the appropriate poem from those available in this volume or compose your own.

Please Write ...

A Single Word

For many days, I have not heard
From you, my love, a single word;
Have you forgotten I exist,
Or did you break your writing wrist?

-♥-

Silence

The silence of your pen
Makes me deaf with despair;
Causing me to fear
That you no longer care.

-♥-

My Bridge

Your letters were my only bridge,
To a world I cannot see;
And when you stopped,
My bridge collapsed,
In a heap of agony.

Step #8: Handwrite the poem that you selected or composed onto the inside of the card using a black ink pen.

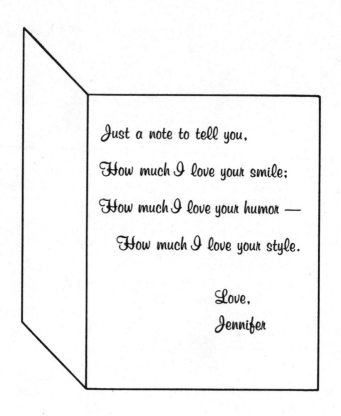

Variation: If you wish, you may print the poem instead of handwriting it.

APPENDIX B/Examples of Love Letters
With Poem Inserts

Introduction

A love poem is a very powerful method of expression. In addition to standing on its own, it can be used to highlight a particular emotion, sentiment or idea when used within a letter.

Each one of the following six love letters deals with a different situation and incorporates a poem or several poems in the body of the text. The topics are: 1) Beginnings, 2) Friendship, 3) Declarations of Love, 4) The Pain of Separation, 5) Reconcilliation, and 6) The Reaffirmation of Love.

All of these love letters are presented for your use. Modify them to suit your own specialized needs or use them as is if they fit your particular situation.

Love Letter No. 1

(Beginnings)

Dear (*Name*):

I bet you thought you wouldn't hear from me so soon - or maybe you thought you wouldn't hear from me at all. Well, You lost! I had a few moments to spare, so I thought I'd make good use of them.

In all honesty, (*Name*), I'm not a very smooth talker and often I have a difficult time finding the right words with which to express my true feelings. But this time, I just had to give it a try. Sure, I could have called you, but I thought I'd write instead.

(*Name*), Ever since we met, I've been thinking of you. I can't ignore the fact that you exist, because in our few hours together, you made an impression on me that will last for a long, long time.

The other day I saw a book of poetry and in it I found a poem which I liked. I changed it around just a little to express how I feel. It's short and to the point, and I hope it (*echoes/expresses*) your thoughts as well.

A Chance Encounter

A chance encounter of the best kind —
A meeting arranged by fate;
Whatever you choose to call it,
I think we should celebrate!
So come with me next Friday night
And get to know me more;
We'll eat and drink beneath the stars,
And laugh while we explore.

Call me at (*Phone number*) if you agree.

Your friend,

(*Name*)

Love Letter No. 2

(Friendship)

Dear (*Name*):

    I hope this letter finds you (*well/in good spirits*). (*Even though I saw you recently,/It's been a while since we last spoke, so*) I thought I'd write you a letter to tell you what's been on my mind for (*some/a long*) time.

    (*Name*), I know a lot of people and feel fortunate to have many good friends, but you are something special. A few weeks ago I came across a poem which expresses exactly how I feel about you. It's short but it's packed with a lot of meaning. So (*Name*), as they say, "This poem's for you!"

A Special Friend

You are a true friend who gives me much —
Who's there to listen - Who's there in a clutch;
A friend like you is rare indeed —
A Godsend and a special breed.

    (*Name*), your friendship truly does mean a great deal to me. I hope that I will always be favored with it, and above all, remain worthy of it.

(*Name*)

Love Letter No. 3

(Declarations of Love)

Dearest (*Name*):

> What would the Yin be without the Yang —
> What would lemon pie be without the meringue?
> What would false be without true —
> And what would I be without you?

(*Name*), the very thought of living my life without you is unbearable, for you are an inseparable part of me. You give to me an inner strength to meet each day. You make me laugh and you bring joy and happiness to my life.

Without you, I would truly be less than whole. For you are the positive to my negative - you bring out all that is good in me. You are the topping of my life - You add a touch of anticipation to each day and much excitement to each night. You show me the true possibilities - the big picture - and make me work harder to reach my potential. But most of all, you are my partner, my pal, and the greatest love of my life!

(Name)

Love Letter No. 4

(The Pain of Separation)

Dearest (*Name*):

> To you, I must confess
> I miss you very much!
> I miss your kiss! I miss your hug!
> I miss your tender touch!

Our separation has been very difficult for me to take, for I do miss you very much. In fact,

> I can't enjoy a lonely meal,
> Nor music do I wish to play,
> For my life has lost all its color,
> With you so far away.

And then there are those long lonely nights without you. I cope with them the only way I can —

> At night, I lie in bed awake,
> And think of all your many charms;
> And dream of the day when I will be
> Back safe in your loving arms.

(*Name*), You are my strength - my light at the end of the tunnel - my pot of gold at the end of the rainbow. Just knowing that you are there waiting for me helps me to carry on.

In closing, I send to you with this note my deepest love and most passionate kiss.

Eternally,

(*Name*)

Love Letter No. 5

(Reconcilliation)

Dear (*Name*):

What can I say to express to you how badly I feel about what happened between us? It is as if a small, insignificant stone tumbling down a mountainside caused a huge, devastating avalanche - an avalanche which took a great personal toll. I am convinced that you and I are the victims of such an avalanche.

(*Name*), I am sick with despair. You have not spoken to me since our disagreement. You won't even return my calls. It's as if you have blotted me out of your life. I cannot undo what was said, nor can I force you to open up to me. I can only tell you that I learned much from this experience. I learned that in the heat of passion many things can be said that cloud and muddle the subject at hand. Upon some reflection, I learned that there can be two sometimes equally valid ways of looking at things, and most important of all, I learned that, often, only when one loses or is about to lose an important part of one's life, does one then realize its true significance and value.

(*Name*), you are very special to me, so in closing I want to leave you with a poem I found which expresses my feelings at this difficult time in my life.

> Sometimes words can be obstacles,
>   As real as any mountain chain,
> Or raging river running swift;
>   Sometimes words can cause great pain
> And create a lovers' rift;
>   But words can also fix bridges and heal wounds;
> Words can spirits lift;
>   And so with this verse, I send
> My sincerest lover's gift —
>   To cause the pain you feel to end;
> To right the wrong of words untrue;
>   From my heart - three words to mend;
> And they are simply - "I Love You!"

(*Name*)

Love Letter No. 6

(Reaffirmation of Love)

Dearest (*Name*):

I thought I'd write you a letter to express how I feel. Now, I know you'll probably think it silly of me to do so, especially since we (*live together/see each other regularly*). But (*Name*), through a letter I can say exactly what's on my mind and in my heart. I know that through the years I haven't been the most verbal or articulate person you've ever known. And Lord knows, I've (*been remiss in expressing/neglected to express*) to you in words my love and affection, even though I feel my actions proved without a doubt that it did exist and still does. Wouldn't you know it, I'm rambling on without saying what I set out to say. And to make matters worse I forgot how I was going to say it.

Oh, wait! All hope is not lost. Yesterday, I was reading a book of poetry and in it I found a poem which surprisingly enough expresses how I feel. (*Name*), even though I did not write it, please think of it as coming from me - from my heart to yours.

> How can I describe what you are to me?
> Mere words do you no justice —
> For you are an infatuation which does not end —
> A fascination of the nth degree —
> A passion which consumes all thought and deed
> And fills my life with poetry!

Love eternally,

(*Name*)

APPENDIX C/Selected Love Symbols
For Cards and Letters

Introduction

The following selected Love Symbols are presented for your use. You may photocopy them on white or colored paper and then cut them out for placement on your personalized greeting card. You may want to trace them directly onto a blank greeting card so that the illustration looks hand-drawn. Last but not least, you may wish to use a part of a love symbol as a beginning to a more complex illustration which you can then photocopy or draw directly onto a blank card. As in the case of the love poems, the variations are endless.

Selected Love Symbols

XOXOXOXOXOXO
XOXOXOXOXOXO
XOXOXOXOXOXO
XOXOXOXOXOXO
XOXOXOXOXOXO
XOXOXOXOXOXO
XOXOXOXOXOXO
XOXOXOXOXOXO

Selected Love Symbols

Selected Love Symbols

Index

A

Ache, 41
Acorn, 39
Actions, 37
Adore, 15
Affair, 6
Affection, 21
Agony, 19,35
Alone, 24,59
Ambrosia, 54
Angel, 38
Anticipation, 14
Apart, 18,49
Arms, 12,23,25,40,
   50,55,64
Art, 60
Autumn, 10

B

Beacon, 30
Beauty, 11,23,51-52,59
Beginnings, 1,73
Best, 47,57
Better, 57
Blessed, 43
Bliss, 29
Bluebells, 43
Blue(s), 39,47-48
Body, 25,62
Bouquet, 30
Bridge, 35,56
Buddy, 8
Butterfly, 4,64

C

Candle, 13,20
Care, 6,34-35,48
Caress, 61
Caring, 8,45,50,54
Carnations, 43
Celebrate, 4
Celebration, 14
Certainty, 27
Chance, 4
Charming, 50,55
Charms, 11,23,25,58
Cheer, 48
Cheerful, 21
Clouds, 37
Combination, 40
Complete, 29
Compromise, 28
Comrade, 8,57
Confess, 18
Confessed, 37
Contentment, 31,58
Cute, 64

D

Daffodil, 4
Darkness, 48
Date, 26
Day, 9,27,39,45-47,
   58,62-63
Debonaire, 53
Declarations of Love, 75
Defences, 4
Dejection, 21
Delight, 30,60-62
Delightful, 45,64
Dependency, 20
Depend, 7
Depressed, 47
Desire, 19
Despair, 35,48,63
Devoted, 33,45
Diamond, 30,54
Disarming, 55
Divine, 6,50,63
Do You Care?, 6
Dream, 14,25,62

E

Earth, 40,47,52,61
Earthquake, 5
Ecstacy, 21,55-56
Embrace, 5,13,21-22,59,
   61,63-64
Emptiness, 17
Encounter, 4
Endure, 31
Energy, 25
Eternity, 19
Excitement, 4
Exciting, 33
Exploration, 55
Explore, 4
Eyes, 23,51-52,54,59,64

F

Face, 3,13,21,60-61,64
Faith, 9,32,34
Fascination, 21,55
Feelings, 5,23,39-40,63
Figure, 59
Fire(s), 19,24
Flair, 53
Flame, 13,30
Flowers, 10,53
Forgive, 31
Forgiveness, 32,24,49
Force field, 29
Friend, 7-8
Friendship, 7-8,32,36,74
Fulfillment, 20
Future, 39

G

Gardenias, 44
Gentle, 54
Gift, 30,33,42
Giving, 7
Glorious, 45
God, 9,30,34,43,47,49
Godsend, 7
Good, 57
Grace 23

H

Happiness, 11,20,23,27,
   54,56,58,62
Happy Birthday, 47
Handsome, 43,50,60-61,64
Heal, 41
Health, 27,47
Heart(s), 5,15-17, 19,24
   30-31,33,36-37,39-42
   46,49,57-60,62-64
Heaven, 51
Heaven-made, 30
Herbs and spices, 32
Honesty, 28,32
Hope for the future, 9
Hour, 13,16
Hug, 18
Humor, 26
Hurt, 41
Husband, 45

I

I Am Happy, 11
I Can't Live..., 13
If I Had A Wish, 12
I Love You, 14-15
I Miss You, 16,18
Incomplete, 13
I Need You, 19
Infatuation, 21
Inspiration, 51
Isolation, 40
I Think Of You, 24
Irresistible, 59

J-K

Jealousy, 34
Joy, 5,9-11,41,50,61,64
Just A Note, 26
Keepsake, 48
Key, 56
Kind, 7,55
Kiss, 13,18,47,50,64

L

Let's Not Argue, 28
Letters, 35-36,39
Life, 16,29,50,57,61,63-64
Light, 30,46
Lips, 54,59,63
Living, 62
Loneliness, 20,24
Lonely, 16,61
Love, 5,6,11,14,20,23,25
27-28,30-34,37-39,41-42
45,47-50,58,61-62
Loving, 45,54
Love Is..., 29
Love Letters, 71
Lovely, 23,43,51-52,60-61,64
Lovers, 24
Love Symbols, 79
Loyal, 7
Loyalty, 27,32
Lust, 32

M

Magnet(s), 58-59
Magnolias, 44
Meaning, 63
Medicine, 48
Meeting, 4
Miles, 18,22,33
Millionaire, 63-64
Mind(s), 16, 24-25,31,36
55,58-59
Misery, 20
Mistake, 41
Mountains, 40

N-O

Nectar, 4
Need(s), 50
News, 36
Night, 3,18,25,46-48,54,61
Obstacles, 42
Ocean, 19,22
One-of-a-kind, 54
Opposites, 58
Orchids, 44
Our Love Is Strong, 33

P

Pain, 18,20,42
Pain Of Separation, 76
Paradise, 63
Passages, 36
Passion(s), 11,19,21,
24-25,40
Pathways, 40
Patience, 5,32
Pearls, 57
Perfect, 57
Perfection, 21
Personalized Expression, 65
Personalized Greeting Cards, 65
Pleasant, 64
Please Write, 35
Pleasure, 30,60

P (cont'd)

Poetry, 21
Point of view, 25
Potpourri, 37
Power, 58
Prayer, 55
Precious, 55
Priceless, 49
Prize, 54
Protect, 29
Purity, 39

Q-R

Rare, 7,53,55
Reaffirm, 50
Reaffirmation of Love, 78
Reconcilliation, 41,77
Refined, 33
Reflection, 21
Rendezvous, 12,18,24
Renew, 60
Respect, 28-29,32
Reunite, 12
Rivers, 5
Rose, 54
Roses Are Red, 43-44

S

Sacrifices, 27
Sad, 9
Sculpture, 31
Sea, 38,40,46,57
Seasons, 64
Second, 13
Selfishness, 34
Sensation, 62
Senses, 37, 62
Separation, 25
Serene, 31
Sexy, 21
Sharing, 50
Sight, 3,43,60,64
Sighs, 23
Silence, 35-36
Sincere, 6,33,54
Skies, 36
Sky, 61-62
Smile, 26,51
Soothing, 61
Soul(s), 29,31,54
Special, 7,14,30,45,47,54
Special Ocassions, 45
Specialty, 37
Spirit(s), 25,39,48,60-61
Spring(s), 5,9,30,53
Stars, 4
Stimulation, 55
Storms, 34
Strength, 58
Stress, 20,61
Style, 26
Success, 27,54
Summer, 10
Sun, 54
Sunshine, 61
Supreme, 14
Symphony, 31

T

Taste, 9
Temptation, 55
Test, 37
Thought(s), 18,24-25,28
40,47,58-59,61
Thoughtful, 7
Thrilled, 37
Thrill(s), 10,50
Time, 9,62
Timeless, 37
To Cheer You Up, 48
Tommorrow, 9
Tonight, 44,48
Touch, 18,22,61
Traveler, 41
Treat, 47
Troubles, 9,39
Trust, 28,31-32,34

U-V

Understand, 31
Understanding, 28,55
Ultimate, 14
Unique, 49,54
Unselfish, 33
Valentine, 49-50
Valentine's Day, 49
Verse, 47-48
Vibration, 62
Vision, 3,16,18,24,61
Vows, 40

W

Warm, 55,61
Wealth, 27
Whole, 20,29
Wife, 45
Wilderness, 56
Windows, 36
Wings, 62
Winter, 9
Wish, 12,27,45,47
Wit, 23
Woman, 32
Words, 36,39,42,57,59
World, 11,30,34-35,43
50,56,62
Write, 36
Writing, 35

X-Y-Z

You Are Beautiful, 51
You Are Special, 53
You Are The Best, 57
You Attract Me, 58
Year, 45-47
Yearning, 41
You Make Me Feel Good, 60

Other Books And Educational Products From The Electric Press

Now Available

Alphabet Twist®

The most versatile educational card game currently available. 108 cards with four complete alphabets in four color suits permit the playing of many interesting alphabet and word games. Rules for **Alphabet Twist®**, **Alphabet Run**™, **Letter Link**™ and **LetteRoundup**™ are included. The enclosed Parent-Teacher Guide provides techniques to teach phonics, letter sequencing, and basic word construction. **Alphabet Twist®** is a great way to teach the alphabet and at the same time help a child develop basic decision-making and critical-thinking skills. It is also excellent for ESL and remedial English students.

Available Fall 1988

Rinky Dink® (Revised Edition)

A simple yet challenging card game utilizing 104 special playing cards with a circus theme. **Rinky Dink®** is an excellent educational-entertainment card game which will provide hours of wholesome enjoyment for both children as well as adults.

Soon To Be Released

Word Wonder™

The Ultimate Word Game!

Phonics Fever™

The Ultimate Phonics Game!

Numbo™

The Ultimate Arithmetic Game!

Order Form

(May Be Photocopied)

Name:_____

Address:_____

City: _____ State:_____ Zipcode:_____

Purchase Order No. (School,State,Fed. orders only):_____

Telephone:_____ Area Code:_____

Ordered By:_____

Ship To:_____

Address:_____

City: _____ State:_____ Zipcode:_____

Attention:_____

Please send me/us the following items:

Qty	Description	Each	Total
_____	__ Love Poems (0-916919-60-9)__	$4.95	_____
_____	__ Pearls of Love (0-916919-00-5)_____	$9.95	_____
_____	__ Alphabet Twist® (EP86EG001)_____	$9.95	_____
_____	__ Rinky Dink® (EP88EG002)_____	$4.95	_____
	Subtotal_____		_____
	State Sales Tax (Calif. Residents Only)_____		_____
	15% Postage and Handling_____		_____
	Total Amount_____		_____

Enclosed, please find a ☐ Check ☐ Money Order in
the amount of $_____ to cover the order, sales tax if
required, and 15% for postage.

☐ Please bill me/us - See Purchase Order No. above
(School, State, Federal institutions only).

The Electric Press
Mail-Order Department
P.O. Box 6025
Fresno, California 93703

About The Author

Ara John Movsesian was born on June 16, 1949, in Troy, New York. In 1955, he and his parents moved to California and settled in Fresno where he spent his childhood and adolescence. In 1969, Ara entered the University of California at Berkeley from where, in 1974, he graduated with a Masters Degree in Architecture. Today, he is a licensed architect specializing in residential and commercial design. To him, his vocation as an Architect and avocation as a writer and poet are interrelated endeavors. "One cannot separate Writing - a romantic and creative process from Architecture - a visionary profession. They both require inspiration, technical ability, and discipline." In 1983, Ara wrote his first book entitled **Pearls of Love: How To Write Love Letters and Love Poems**. Over the years it has become one of the most recognized works on the topic of romantic writing and communication. It has even been called a modern-day version of Cyrano de Bergerac. **Love Poems** *for Cards and Letters* is his second book. In it he presents his poetry as a powerful and effective method of expressing and communicating friendship and love in all of its many forms.